BENEATH OUR FEET

Mel McMahon

Abbey Press
2018

First published in 2018

Abbey Press
77A, Ashgrove Road
Newry
Co Down
BT34 1QN
N Ireland

LOTTERY FUNDED

© Mel McMahon, 2018

Layout and cover design:
Don Hawthorn / David Anderson / Adrian Rice
Typesetting by David Anderson in 11/14.5pt Sabon
Printed by Nicholson & Bass Ltd, Belfast

A catalogue record for this book is available from the British Library

ISBN: 978-1-909751-81-1

To the memory of Wilfred Owen,
Killed in action,
Ors, France,
4th November, 1918

Biographical Note

Mel McMahon was born in Lurgan in 1968. His work has appeared widely in journals and anthologies and has been broadcast on BBC Radio Ulster. He has been short-listed for several literary prizes and was a prize-winner in the FSNI Poetry Competition (2015). His work has been nominated twice for the Forward Prize for best individual poem. His first collection, *Out of Breath,* was published by Summer Palace Press in 2016. He is currently Head of English at the Abbey Grammar School, Newry, County Down.

Acknowledgements

A version of 'Shrapnel Pieces' was first broadcast by Lagan Online in 2018.

My thanks to Damian Smyth, Catherine Walker MBE (Curator of the War Poets' Collection, Napier University), Angélique Labiouse (Forester's Cellar near Ors), Mark Roper, Adrian Rice, Adrian Bradley, Colin Dardis, Geraldine Dardis O'Kane, Amy Wyatt Rafferty, Paul Rafferty, Tom Kelly, Charlie Heaney, Mary Heaney, Eugene Kielt, Gerardine Kielt, Sean Sloan, Gerald Morgan, Kate Newmann, Joan Newmann, Paula Meehan, Ross Thompson, Lynda Tavakoli, Csilla Toldy, Lucy Elder, Keith Acheson, Malachi Kelly, Carole Delcambre, Theo Dorgan, Sir Ken and Lady Terry Robinson, Ross Wilson, Arthur Ward, Philip Orr, the Patrons of Abbey Press, Marion Clarke, Jacky Duminy (Mayor of Ors), Jeanne-Marie Dineur, Dr. Jane Potter, Sandra Powlette and Peter and Elizabeth Owen.

The author gratefully acknowledges receipt of a SIAP grant from the Arts Council of Northern Ireland which was instrumental in the completion of this project.

I am also permanently grateful to Bernadette, Claire and Mark for giving me the time and space in which to write.

Manuscript of "The Send Off" on front cover by permission of The British Library and The Wilfred Owen Estate, image via The First World War Digital Archive, University of Oxford http://www.owcs.ox.ac.uk/ww1lit/

Contents

Mother / 11

Signing Up / 11

Guard Duty (London) / 12

Calling Time / 12

War / 12

France 1917 / 13

Pals' Batallions / 13

Some Others / 14

The Names / 14

Thoughts on Keats / 15

To the Reader / 15

Shelter / 16

Routine / 16

Sides / 17

No Poets / 17

A Soldier's Fear / 18

Spring / 18

Remembering the Somme / 19

Prayer / 19

Bones / 20

Dilemma / 20

The Catch / 21

Music / 21

Verse / 22

In the Trenches / 22

Sight Lines / 23

Dream / 24

The Dying / 25

Chaplain / 25

The Generals / 26

Caps / 26

Mother's Letters / 27

House Martens / 27

Desertion / 28

The Men / 28

Books / 29

Letters / 29

The Fallen / 30

Greater Love / 30

From the Front / 31

Bluebottles / 32

Lost Covenant / 33

Raspberries / 33

Craiglockhart / 34

Tynecastle Primary School / 40

Sick Leave / 41

Ripon / 42

Barbed Wire / 42

Bells / 43

Turret Room, Scarborough / 44

Father's Pride / 45

The Firestep / 46

Camouflage / 46

Skin / 47

Beyond / 47

Undertaker / 47

Fatigue / 48

Winter at War / 49

Erased / 50

Older / 51

Return / 51

Peace / 51

Rhythms / 52

Urn / 52

Last Post / 53

The Future / 53

Abide With Me / 53

Over / 54

Days Like These / 54

Shrapnel Pieces / 55

To the Young / 60

Telegram / 61

End / 62

BENEATH OUR FEET

1915

Mother

To see you stand at the door and wave
Until I have passed from view
Puts heart in my stride that will pave
Return, to get back, back, back to you.

Signing Up

Signing papers to go to war
Felt formal, even truant.
Running away – but in uniform,
A sense of adventure ruined.

Guard Duty (London)

Tonight I stand on guard.
My thoughts, lazy and slow,
Long for the arrival of letters
As I watch the jiggering snow.

Calling Time

Two lovers at a train station
Hold each other tight.
Like hands of a town clock
Finding home at midnight.

War

A word like war, so small,
So long unheard, unseen.
Against it, words like love and hope
Smash to smithereens.

France 1917

Beneath our feet, this sucking mud
Makes waste of flowers and trees.
Nature is strangled; has lost its power.
Mud clings to our boots with rotting flesh.
Each step brings a slucking squelch.
The ground seems to gasp, expire.

Pals' Batallions

We have played cheek by jowl,
Lived our lives on kindred streets.

Wherever our spirits are sent to dwell
We do so together: fearful; complete.

Some Others

There were the Scottish regiments
Who wore their kilts to war.
In winter, the starched hem of their tartan
Ran its blade along their legs: red; raw.

The Names

Before the war each town had streets
And nearby fields had names.
By the time this fighting is complete
What will be left to claim?

Thoughts on Keats

And maybe, when a poet dies,
Amidst the sorrow, the unwept cries,
The freed spirit leaves and seeks out more.

And what if, as it travels light
Seeking what it knows as right,
The heart it seeks as home is yours?

To the Reader

How many thoughts within the mind
Have yet to be said or penned?
I write these poems as letters
And hope to find in readers, friends.

Shelter

At night we seek out ways
To still the tired and wrestling mind.
I turn to verse; sometimes prayers.
Boulders to hide behind.

Routine

In the morning, the thumping noise of bombs.
We see no birds nor hear them sing.
At night, bombardments like thunderstorms.
Air crazed with loveless lightning.

Sides

I
Hail the German who fights for life
Through the wounds and death and stench,
The man who writes by the dimmest light
Poems in another trench!

II
And what if in all of this
I kill a soldier just like me?
Deprive a father, mother, sister
Of his love, his words, his poetry?

No Poets

No matter how many attack the page
To end the day, before they rest,
Ink cannot drown a poet's rage;
No line guard life or give the fallen breath.

A Soldier's Fear

When battle starts I will be lost
In debris, smoke and sound.
Keep safe the words I write.
My body may not be found.

Spring

Spring arrives but nothing buds.
No sense of rise or birth.
Up and down French fields in rows,
Soldiers: dead seeds in fertile earth.

Remembering the Somme

What lines do I write after battle
With the blunt head of an ailing pen?
The fallen lie scattered in fields. To write
About land, lost or gained,
Is to plough through the flesh of men.

Prayer

Beyond the cries of boys,
Beyond the tears of men,
Lost somewhere in a glar of mud
Lies a prayer with no 'Amen'.

Bones

What does war care for who we are?
Whether we have a father, a mother?
Where we fall we may lie to rot.
Who can tell one man's bones from another's?

Dilemma

Lucky to zig-zag bullets for days,
Volleys of whispers caught the boy
And took him in their fire:
He can't shoot; he doesn't want
To cut these bastards down to size.
True. Easier to miss bullets
Than to send one through the air:
To look a dying soldier in the eyes.

The Catch

The shelled land shakes off
Its dust of brief concussion.
Fresh shells tear the air and fall.
Numbed land, numbed air,
Numb feet, numb hands –
Hands too numb to curl fingers,
To pull triggers, to beckon death,
To stare a soldier in the face
And not see days when he was held
By a parent, a grandparent,
When the very mention of his name
Raised a smile, a lift of breath.

Music

Our trenches stretch for miles
And dwindle out of sight.
We have turned the land to staves.
What music shall we write?

Verse

When I wake each morning it comes to mind
The poems that the day might give.
Around me the men whose deaths may find
Space in verse when they ought to live.

In the Trenches

Long now in the trenches
Our ears are finely tuned
For bombs. We scurry below ground
Like maggots writhing in a wound.

Sight Lines

His eyes had gone sour.
The optic nerves, dead roots.
Like small onions gone bad
They were scooped out and scrapped.
The hollowed spaces that they left
Made giant gashes, ugly.
We stitched his lids with thread,
Entombed him in his darkness
With clumsy needlework.

His skull, unable to be lit by any light,
Pulsed now with sounds.
The world became a puzzle
In which he sensed out steps.

They said he could hear a whisper
As it was being thought.

Dream

Unslept for days, the night filled with shells,
Our bodies marred by pain: the pain of hunger,
The pain of noise, the pain of shrunken space –
I looked across to No Man's Land
And saw its ground lit up;
Shapes scooped by bombs
That could have been
The letters of soldiers' names
Carved out on tombstones
In far off churchyards,
Unreadable, spilling over with rain.

The Dying

A soldier lies, unable to move
Beneath the midday sun.
The air is ravenous with flies
Circling to slurp on his stomach's sluice.
Soon what will be left of him
Will be bones, wisps of hair to wreathe
The violation of skull, its shocked orbits,
The exposed jaw's cartridge of flashing teeth.

Chaplain

When you close your eyes at night
Do you see Heaven? Do you feel Hell?
That depends, Father, on what I hear last:
The snores of men; the screams of shells.

The Generals

When you hear of the numbers dead
Do you sip your tea and sigh
Before taking out maps to plan ahead
Where next we will bleed and die?

Caps

The caps we wore showed rank,
Declared what we could eat
And where that we could lie.
They determined when we'd leave
The trench, on which part
Of the field we'd die.

Mother's Letters

The arrival of her letters
Always brings me peace,
Makes the noise around me stop.

Her words move like pilgrims
Along the unlined route
Of our shared heart's codeless map.

House Martens

At home the martens return:
They spiral, twist and dive.
And with them comes hope.
For last year they were there,
Have now returned, are still alive.

Desertion

Fatigued and tired of battle
He could hide in the woods
And find, there, sanctuary
For his mind's deep wounds.
The broken branches
Hanging like oars
Could row him deeper, further,
From those angry afternoons.

The Men

Here there is no room for lust.
Another's touch I do not miss.
Friendship gathers us in its clutch.
Our shared quiet intimate as a kiss.

Books

What good does it do
To write down words anew,
When old words given
By poets and sages
Hide in books' unopened pages
As if obeying curfew?

Letters

As the others sleep I stay awake
And seek encounter with the page.

Not wanting to stir the men
I scratch down words to catch the day.

There is nobility in their aching frames,
Cut skin, scorched flesh and restless bones.

Hidden like a dark secret underground,
Breathing corpses, lost and far from home.

The Fallen

What could exceed this,
This grey-grim theatre of pain?
The body grieves seeing bones
That can never love again.

Greater Love

Who would not feel for the man
Who toils beside him,
Selfless to the end?
Or admire the strength in limbs
Loved at home under kinder suns?
No place, no time to think him a lover
When he muscles a path across
Tattered lines. You watch him go, a brother,
Thrown into war's pitch and toss.
Fear torches the desire that's felt.
Deeper love lies buried with the bones
Beneath war's filth and excrement.

From the Front

Dear Mother,
             I have just risen from bed
To write these lines, a letter too long delayed.
So many nights I've lain down here and prayed
To hear your voice, not the sounds of air being flayed
By bullet and bomb. War has made
A hell of all we know. We have strayed
So far from what was once ourselves; it has led
Us down paths from which we might not tread
Back. Yet, if these nights and days can pay
Our debts and end despair, so be it. We will have bled
But not in vain. What I have heard and read
Here in the lives of others has weighed
Down my heart so that I, too, have felt dead, undead.

But I smile thinking of you, us.
                            Your own,
                                    Wilfred.

Bluebottles

I

The wind blew fierce that day,
Fanned us with terrible heat.
A bluebottle bolted and buzzed in my mouth
Having fed on the sour soup of guts
Open in our many dead.
Inside my mouth I taste strange meat.

II

The flies that buttoned themselves to uniforms
And tacked themselves to a soldier's face
Will return in spring having found
For winter a quiet and bomb-free space.

III

Are we any different to flies
Whose buzz engulfs our marching men?
Despite our flicks and swipes they come
At us again and again and again.

IV

Bluebottles come in squadrons
Seeking the surrender of men as meat.
We sweat our way down ruined roads
And curse them each day. Repeat. Repeat. Repeat.

V

A man cut down in no-man's land
Will soon be dead as stone.
Within nine days the flies will strip
His body back to bone.

Lost Covenant

Half-awake in these trenches
We feel like bait within a trap.
Can the dove bring us its olive branch?
Has God lost His compass and map?

Raspberries

Everywhere – sunshine and
The blood of fallen men.
Stupidly I think of summer. Raspberries.
And wish I was home again.

Craiglockhart

On 25th June, 1917, Wilfred Owen arrives to recuperate in Craiglockhart Military Hospital, Edinburgh, after suffering shellshock in France. Here he meets Siegfried Sassoon and is treated by Dr. Brock, a pioneer in ergotherapy.

Sleep

In darkness I smoke by candlelight.
The night kisses silence with doom.
How I long to hear the chat of men,
Soldiers snoring in other rooms!

By day the soldiers get lost in talk
With those who seem to care.
At night the building goes to war
And becomes a sepulchre.

Ergotherapy

At last I have been given work to do
To push my research to the brink.
I must forget mosses that swell nearby
As I ponder on: 'Do Plants Think?'

Swimming Pool

I have found friendship here with others.
In these streets, I feel, we thrive.
But some days I refuse the open space
To lose myself in water: briefly feel alive.

The Field Club

Today we walk in the Pentland Hills
With so much knowledge out on show.
One, an expert on birds, another on bees;
A padre knowing nothing. Myself? Incognito.

Exits

We are here until we learn how
To order the chaos of our inner mess.
Some will find poetry
Some will find paint.
Some will exit high windows –
Explosions of glass and flesh.

On Meeting Sassoon

I
He sat polishing his golf clubs
When I entered, and remained unfussed.
He took my book to sign his work:
Diamonds he'd found in the darkest dust.

II
I could see pain and grief
Writhe in the depths of his eyes.
To talk to him at last
Was more than meeting another man
And speaking face-to-face.

He told me my poems
Yet had horrors to embrace.

III
A mad comet of sorts, I have been from the start.
When death comes, know this:
You have fixed my life – however short.

Robert Graves

I

I met him rarely. Though very plain,
He knew Sassoon. I know he saw
My poems. He later wrote, saying,
Puff out your chest...outlive the war.

II

With a ruined lung
He was sent home to heal,
To sit outside in the sun.
He swathed his feet
In the swishing grass.
But in his garden
Where insects droned
There came sometimes
Strange smells from flowers,
Then not flowers, but gas, gas, gas!

Dr. Brock

At times we speak until midnight.
We talk to give space to war.
My dreams are no longer in trenches,
Merely death met by motor car.

He sends me to the Slum Gardens
And I feel forced to give consent.
To ground me I now must meet
Edinburgh's submerged one tenth.

Recovery

How easy now it is to search
For rhymes with flowers or trees.
In war, words lie choked in ruts,
And chime with miseries.

Gas Poem

Stronger with every breath I feel
Closer and closer to home.
But at nights these wards
Spark wild with shells –
My pen gasps for my gas poem.

A Painting

Looking out from a trench
Smoke lifts on clear blue skies.
Men hug mugs of tea. The day fairs.
In this painting no one dies.

Wilfred Owen is discharged from Craiglockhart Military Hospital on 30th October, 1917. He is given three weeks leave before returning to his reserve unit.

Tynecastle Primary School

I visited again at Christmas
And saw my name chalked across their board.
They made me cards and gave me thanks.
Their welcome put my ego to the sword.

Sick Leave

I
Arriving home to a quiet house,
To clean clothes and decent food.

Each night, scorched awake from sleep
By bonfires in the blood.

II
When I lift this glass
To my lips and sip
On wine so dark and red
I close my eyes
And in my head
I cross vineyards,
Pruned and so exact.
Strings of streams
Shoelace the land.
Life is wrapped in sunshine,
Present and correct.

III
Waking up on leave I hear birds sing.
Their notes swell and swirl in circles.
I have a feeling most sublime.
Like trying to read several pages
Of favourite books all at the same time.

Ripon

Outside my cottage window the children play.
They play at being us and in the war.
I look out at their laughter and I pray
Their eyes never see what these eyes saw.

Barbed Wire

Barbed wire fences hem the roads
That I daily walk upon.
Each twist of steel makes me think
Of Arras, Cambrai, Somme.

Bells

Autumn returns
And its soothing air
Takes me in its spell.

On the ground amongst
The fallen leaves
A fuchsia's fallen bell.

Turret Room, Scarborough

I
Despite the laughter and the English air,
Despite my sense that things are well,
I must recall the war, asleep – awake,
Take notes from its searing Hell.

II
The wind turned in the night.
The fire smoked with extra flames.
I stared, I smelt the air
And was transported back to war.

Father's Pride

He saw my months on leave
Close to a waste of time.
Injured men should seek the Front –
Fall quickly back in line.

*Wilfred Owen returns to war in France
in August, 1918.*

The Firestep

Our hearts balloon and shrink on the firestep.
It is a cliff-edge of chance, a dungeon of dare.
Mist cloaks us in its chasuble.
The whistle to charge is a kind of prayer.

Camouflage

Mud cobbles the bodies of fallen men
So in their uniforms they can't be found.
Churned up clots in slurps of mud,
Their blood feeds the sterile ground.

Skin

My skin has become a parchment
Sealed in dust and strangest dirt.
My eyes are murky panes of glass
Hiding rooms of death and hurt.

Beyond

The fighting gives me poems but takes
Men's lives by night and day.
Words weep and hang fatigued.
A hell beyond hyperbole.

Undertaker

With each dip and lift of my pen
I record the war. I
Become undertaker of days,
The passing of men.

Fatigue

I have had enough of war:
The pounding guns;
Noise after noise;
The constant, constant toil.
I yearn to lie this body
Down for sleep
Beneath the blanket
Of this foreign soil.

Winter at War

I
On one of the wood's last trees a robin blazes into song.
You won't catch me! it cries to man, to bullet, to bomb.

II
I can hear the guns stutter as I turn my head for sleep.
I dig for the silences of youth, to embrace, to keep.

III
So cold at night a sea of sounds freezes within our ears.
Our eyes glass over; we are beyond the speech of tears.

Erased

Against the soft wall
Of the trench
Despite sunlight
Cracking my lips,
Despite my fear
Of losing fear,
Despite the warm air
Dry-pasting my throat,
I can feel
The *thump, thump, thump,*
The throb of the land
Against my side and back.
For a second,
As my eyes close,
There is peace.
I feel unborn.

Older

Younger, a canal would have tempted me
To wade in and cast a line.
I content myself now in watching
Its watery hold on place, on time.

Return

If bullets and bombs don't find me here
Shall I return to England whole?
What poetry will come, if poetry comes,
From the lost clockwork of the soul?

Peace

Why should peace be sought
And held up now as victory?
What has led to this? Dead trees, dead men
Riddle the land. Hope's choked ossuary.

Rhythms

Are broken: eating, sleeping, waking –
The very sun seems bulled from its orbit!

Tonight, in the briefest quiet,
I hear the drip-drop of water after rain
In the trenches. I think of the footfall
Of pall bearers carrying us to churches
At home in a slow, corpseless, march
Along paths we'll never walk again.

Urn

Whether it be war or peace
Our men and their men die.
The earth is a great urn
In which our ashes lie.

Last Post

The bugle calls and seems to beckon
Lost spirits of those who fell.
The notes form units that search
Out men from nothingness and hell.

The Future

The sun cleanses this morning.
Truth runs fast on a bristling breeze.
Where they now fly, in years to come
Birds will nest high in thick-grown trees.

Abide With Me

Those of you who stand on land
Where we fought and who now see
A calm landscape void of men,
In life, in death, abide with me.

Over

The war is nearly over. The Germans are far through.
Our step quickens. All we have to do
Is take the Ors Canal and not much more.
Mist envelopes morning and pontoons shake –
Gunfire, bullets streaking near. I imagine
My boat home to Dover. I disembark.
News of my return, a surprise at our front door.

Days Like These

This morning my clothes smell of cigarettes,
My ears ring with laughter, the stories of men.
The war is coming to an end.
When shall I know such days again?

Shrapnel Pieces

I

To live in a place without a road,
Without grass or flowers or trees
And realise despair has somehow found
The poet awake in me.

II

Though war has brought us pain,
Kept loved ones out of reach,
It has stormed the gates of silence,
Wrought sad wisdom from our speech.

III

Shells squash hope, suffocate the air,
Put men and land to the highest test.
Where a bush holds a fist of branches
Like fractured bones, inside, intact, a nest.

IV

If I could truly tell the story
Of all of these dead men
It would deafen like the flight of shells
From whence I'd carved my pen.

V
No words I use can catch the weight
Of noise, of smells, the moment when

A life is ended. How light the word 'horror'
In a mouth or slipping from a pen.

VI
To march when tired, a wretched task,
Hauling one leg in front of the other.
All I want now is to hold a pen,
To embrace the words *sweetheart, mother*.

VII
How do we get the rhythms back,
The ones that kept us sane?
In books, in ink, in talk with men
Who face pain after pain after pain?

VIII
How do I, unknown, unseen,
Put pen to a rationed page,
Write words that will upset those men
Who need to taste our rage?

IX

I will work this pen until it finds
A rhythm like a metronome
To take me back to different days,
Far from war and close to home.

X

Standing entombed in trenches,
Smothered in the bombs' dead noise,
Enduring each long and wringing raid,
I recall as a child
How I'd roll my socks in a ball
And hurl them down the landing
Like a soft, benign grenade.

XI

If only I could get to sleep
Amidst this noise and toil.
To waken late as I did in youth:
You'll sleep your brains into engine oil.

XII

Even hunkered in a trench
Begging body and soul to sleep apart
I hear a soldier cleave to words.
His prayer a meteor in the dark.

XIII
Bombs have pilfered from these woods.
What stood for centuries is gone.
And what's been taken from the hearts
Of men will never, ever return.

XIV
Looking across a battlefield
– Bombs shrieking that Hope has failed –
The ground is whipped in welts.
Smoke hangs like sky's entrails.

XV
Each time a man dies in this heat
We bury him near our trench.
We fight on, his body reduced to meat.
Armies of flies parade the stench.

XVI
All is at variance here below
As I think of destiny and fate.
The land is kinetic with death.
Above, the moon, dispassionate.

XVII
The air is tarred with smoke.
Its giant lung clogged with our dirt.
When will madness find its fill?
When will peace salve this hurt?

XVIII
We are slowly dying; the land
Is slowly dying. Nothing takes root.
Battlefields are gulches of fear.
These trenches, ragged scars,
Where pain can't disappear.

To the Young

And do you think war a chance
To kill and be merry?
We fight and we bury.
We fight and we bury.

Telegram

If the telegram comes
I know her world will halt,
And then will blow apart.
Each letter, each embrace we shared,
Lost; the memories of kisses
Torn from inside her heart.

End

How many men did I shoot and kill
From country, village or town?
This morning I genuflect to an unseen bullet
And enter the canal face down.

Wilfred Owen died at the Sambre-Oise Canal in Ors, France, on 4th November, 1918. One week later, as the bells pealed in Shrewsbury to celebrate the Armistice, Owen's mother, Susan, received the telegram informing her of her son's death.